Finding Your Chairs

A NEW APPROACH TO COMMUNICATION

Dan Burrell   Cindy Thomas

Finding Your Chairs

A new approach to communication

Cindy Thomas

ISBN (Print Edition): 979-8-35092-969-0

ISBN (eBook Edition): 979-8-35092-970-6

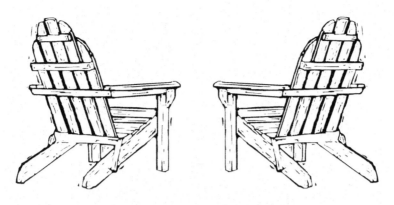

FIRST, THIS IS
WHO WE ARE:

CINDY

The first time I met Dan was in a country club, when we were both work-ing with a local charity. I was two years into a marriage I felt unsure of. Later, I learned that this is a more common experience than what one might imagine. This marriage came after a seven-year relationship, which came after a marriage of twenty-three years.

Something I noticed consistently was the way I always told myself my partner would change. I gave them the benefit of doubt, and assumed that they would eventually evolve into who I hoped they would be, that they would love me the way I wanted to be loved.

I ignored red flags. In my five-year marriage I ignored the fact that I only connected with my partner though golf and travel, but not on an essential emotional level.

The second time I met Dan was at a party that included many of our mutual friends. I had just lost my job of three years and had no intention of going to the party because I was depressed. I found myself at fifty-six, in an unfulfilling marriage, with no outlet. Until then working had been my escape. I decided to go to the party at the last minute.

I looked up and saw him walking towards me. Our eyes met. I knew I had seen him before. He reintroduced himself as Dan from Jersey Mikes, and he immediately asked about my job.

I burst into tears.

"What's next for you?" he asked.

"I have no idea," I said.

He looked at me and said, "this may be the best thing that ever happened to you."

"I have helped some people when they are in this position, Would you like to have lunch sometime and talk about it"? he asked.

He told me that he was essentially interested in helping people find their purpose.

I said yes, but secretly I hoped he had some sort of a job offer for me.

We met for lunch. I truly appreciated his professionalism, the way he listened, and the questions he asked. On some level I was also aware that I didn't, and had never, believed in coincidences. You see.....I am an avid follower of "The Course of Miracles" which allows me to be in touch with the idea that God has me in his plans. A part of me believed that there was a reason I had decided to go to this party, and that God put this man in front of me.

After we chatted some, he said to me, "If I were to wave a magic wand over you and you had 20 seconds to decide what you really wished to do in life, something that you jump out of bed in the morning to go do, what would that be"?

"Clock starts now," he said.

I answered immediately. Dog Rescue or an indoor cycling studio.

He laughed. "Well I don't see much money in the dog rescue, so let's talk about indoor cycling."

Over the next few weeks, Dan and I met regularly to talk about my purpose: to open a cycling studio.

He had been successful in franchising and was a good source of information.

Our connection began slowly, over time, and then suddenly felt immediate. We both felt seen, heard, and supported by each other.

The day that everything changed between us began with a simple text message from Dan: *Would you like to meet for a glass of wine?*

Although I hadn't been feeling well, and had been sick for two weeks, I wanted to meet him.

That evening, I drank tea, he drank wine, we spoke for four hours, walked to the parking lot, and kissed in the pouring rain. I had never felt so loved, so seen, so happy, than I did in that very moment. It was also the first time I had been truly kissed in five years. Soft and slow, with passion and love.

That night, I sent Dan an email: "Thank you for making me feel worthy of a kiss in the rain." He had awakened something inside me that had died. My internal dialogue, as odd as it may sound, was that I would never experience love, that life would be loveless going forward. That moment with Dan changed my outlook.

However, as I drove away that night, I felt a sinking feeling: Dan and I were both married, and neither of us wanted to engage in an affair.

We decided it would be best if we didn't communicate in any form, and so life went on…with no contact for 16 months.

9 months later, I opened my first indoor cycling studio.

I turned inward and buried myself in my work and in my family.

Then the pandemic happened. I worked at the studio each day, alone. I thought about Dan every day, with love, not sadness–I prayed for his happiness. I didn't tell anyone about him.

And then, one day, 16 months after that kiss in the rain, I was in my office, looked up, and saw him standing right in front of me. I felt breathless. For the most part, he and I have been inseparable ever since.

We attribute the beauty and magic of our relationship to a core principle that changed our lives, the very reason we wanted to write this book.

This principle is called: "finding your chairs."

Because of our backgrounds, because of how closely we had observed the failure of our four shared marriages, we knew we had to approach each other with a completely different paradigm, in order to honor how special our connection was. The paradigm is built on radical honesty: **on cultivating the capacity to express oneself with completeness.**

Communication is like an instrument, and this book is an offering on how we have learned to fine-tune our conversations.

The very first step is simple: choose a time to "find your chairs", whenever possible, to sit down, look at your partner, and prepare to tell your truth.

FROM DAN

Three years ago, if you had asked me whether I ever imagined I would be in the kind of relationship I am in now, I would have said: absolutely no way.

The truth is: I used to sit in my backyard, near the edge of the property, meditate, and pray that the relationship I was in would end.

When I first laid eyes on Cindy I thought she was about as beautiful as anyone could be. Her smile was breathtaking. Even though I wasn't looking for a relationship I went up and introduced myself to her. Our conversation was business-like: we spoke about our work and about golf. Three months later I saw her again, at a party at a house on my street. I made a beeline for her immediately, as I was drawn to her smile and to the way she carried herself as she spoke to others.

This time, our conversation turned personal. I had heard that Cindy's job had been terminated, so I asked her what her plans were. She teared up.

"I am not sure," she said. Something about her expression compelled me to ask more questions. Ultimately we decided to finish our conversation over lunch.

We met at a restaurant, where I asked her a question I'd asked many times before:

"If I waved a magic wand over you, and you could do anything in your life, what would you do? You have thirty seconds to answer, what would you change?"

Immediately she said: I would open an indoor cycle studio.

Her answer was clear and made me feel sure that she would accomplish her goal. That seemed to be her purpose and her path.

Today we are business and life partners. We share a beautiful home together–I feel as if the prayer I incanted in my backyard has been answered.

My intention in writing this book is to **share the insights and experiences I have gathered along my life, through a series of relationships, personal growth, and now, through this wonderful partnership with Cindy.** I fundamentally believe that the partnership each one of us longs for is available to anyone, provided **we are willing to tell the truth: first to ourselves, then to others.** The purpose of this book is to lay the foundation for some of these conversations.

A note from the editor: Throughout the next chapters the narrative will be presented from Cindy's point of view, in order to make the tone and story clear to our reader. However, this book and its contents was mutually generated by Dan and Cindy over the course of a year, during which they engaged in conversations that generated the ideas you are about to explore.

TABLE OF CONTENTS

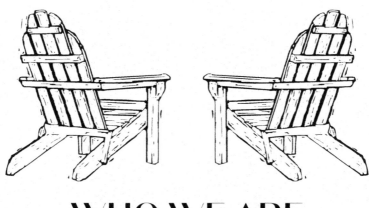

WHO WE ARE

(INTRODUCTION)

If you think about it, we are constantly signing contracts. When you get an apartment, you sign a lease. When you subscribe to Netflix, you agree to pay a set monthly amount. When you rent a car, you sign a document that makes you liable for the vehicle. Similarly, when you get married, or sign a document of domestic partnership, you also enter into an agreement with the person you are going into contract with. Typically, all relationships have moments in which all parties make explicit agreements: to get married, to raise children, to start a business or buy a home. Once these conversations are over, people usually don't revisit them unless something has significantly changed, or unless there is a glaring problem.

The problem, however, is people usually don't revisit the contract of their relationship. They express vows and commitments to each other, and move forward, without the tools to check in to see if their original commitment is still working.

What we have noticed, based on our own experience and speaking with numerous other couples, is that there aren't usually opportunities for additional agreements to be explored, once a relationship is established.

It is almost as if all the mutual agreements are landed on early on, and gradually disappear once a pattern/consensus is established. Because of this, **people don't always get the space they need to re-evaluate and re-create the relationship they desire.** So, our handbook is a tool designed to help you create and/or establish a relationship contract with your partner. Our hope is that this can be useful to you, regardless of whether you have been together a few months, or many years.

It is clear that the traditional structure of marriage and intimate romantic relationships fail more often than they succeed. Every 13 seconds, there is one divorce in America, which equals 277 divorces per hour, 6,646 divorces per day, 46,523 divorces per week, and 2,419,196 divorces per year. This means there are 9 divorces in the time it takes for a couple to recite their wedding vows (2 minutes).[1]

There are many specific stressors that affect intimate relationships, which include: money, children, illness, sex, etc. However, we believe that an additional element is responsible for the disintegration of relationships. Very few of us have a system in place to ascertain whether the agreements we have made in our relationships are working for us, as we change and evolve as people.

So, we are proposing a paradigm shift when it comes to relationships.

We call it.........

"Finding Your Chairs—*a contract to nourish your relationship.*"

---

1   https://www.wf-lawyers.com/divorce-statistics-and-facts/

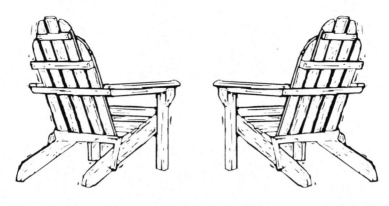

THIS IS WHAT YOU'RE SIGNING UP FOR

(THE CONTRACT)

The premise is simple: you and your partner will decide on an initial period of time or time frame you would like to work on your relationship. If you've just met someone you really like and want to use our program to become closer, you might decide on experimenting with our contract for a month or two. If you have been together for a year or two and are wondering whether you want to invest and continue the relationship long term, you might choose six months. If you've been together for a decade and are interested in increasing your intimacy and becoming closer, you might decide on one year. Regardless of the time frame you choose, it is important that you visualize this time as **an investment into the intimacy and quality of your relationship.** Furthermore, the backdrop of this contract is that you explicitly agree that you have the freedom to walk away from the relationship when your contract comes to an end. If you aren't entirely satisfied with how your month, or three months, or year went, you will agree to have a conversation about what it might look like to end the relationship. The purpose of this is to create a relationship that fills you with joy, honesty, and purpose'. To eliminate the expectation that you or your partner have to settle for anything less than you want or need.

The first step of the relationship contract is to agree to meet at least once a month. This is the practice we call "Finding Your Chairs." Every month you and your partner will sit together, without any distractions, in order to create the practice of vulnerability: of sharing your thoughts and feelings, freely.

These monthly meetings are opportunities to air grievances that ultimately if left unchecked could destroy a relationship, as well as a space to express continued love and dedication. If you already have regular meetings and check ins, this one is not intended to replace them. Rather, this monthly meeting will act as a concentrated space in which you can express and request specific things that will enhance the quality of your connection. Furthermore, this is an opportunity to make sure that your implicit expectations are made explicit, as it is unfair and unrealistic to hold our partners responsible for needs that we don't articulate.

To get started, establish a time and a place in which you have the space and energy to give your partner your undivided attention. You know what undivided attention means right? No phones, computers. Just the two of you.

For this first meeting, you will write two lists. The first list includes qualities that make you feel attracted and drawn to your partner and to the relationship. The second list includes things you might need from your partner. Be specific: this is the time to make note of the small things that mean the most to you, for example, receiving flowers, coming home to a clean house, going out for ice cream, dressing up, going on trips, making new friends together. Make sure to reflect and share the things your partner does (or did, earlier in your relationship) that made/make you feel a spark.

To give you a sense of what we mean, below are the lists we wrote when we first got together.

When Dan wrote a list of the qualities he loved about me, he noted:

My sense of humor

Our communication

The "togetherness" we feel for each other.

Our ability to have fun while doing anything.

The fact that I support the way he is himself.

The fact that Dan trusts I would never intentionally hurt him.

In terms of what Dan needs from me, he wrote:

For me to be honest about how I am feeling, physically and emotionally.

For me to always tell him what I need from him, to make sure expectations are clear.

For me to prioritize my health.

For me to let him help me, and for me to not take on too much.

When I wrote a list of the qualities I loved about Dan, I noted that I loved:

How he takes care of me and makes me feel safe.

The way he makes me feel loved.

The fact that I am attracted to him in every way.

The way we laugh together.

How we are a team, in life and in business.

Traveling together.

The commitment we share toward our families.

The dreams we share.

In terms of what I needs from Dan, I wrote:
Support and advice regarding ongoing business ventures.
Partnership and accountability with physical health practices.
For him to be comfortable being himself with me.

* * *

These lists will vary according to where you are in your life, and what you need. The lists are part of "the relationship agreement," and are intended to act as a living document that you can update or adjust month-to-month. If you can anticipate a particularly rough month ahead, you can take the time to outline which specific gestures might mean the most to you. For example, extra help cooking, cleaning, or planning dates. This is the opportunity for you to listen to your deepest self and articulate the ways you will feel most loved. This way, you can be sure that your partner is investing time and energy into doing things that will be helpful to you. Whatever your specific love language is, make a list of the ways your partner can fulfill this, and present it, as you are "Finding Your Chairs".

The function of these meetings is to promote mutual accountability and transparency in the relationship. We also recommend that you record some of these meetings, with an audio or visual device, in order to create documentation that you can later review if you need to. Each of us carry distinct perceptions about our behavior...... The opportunity to record and review the way we speak gives us the chance to see ourselves anew, each month.

Dan and I filmed our initial commitment to each other while wine tasting, and decided to film many meetings there-after. It gives us an opportunity to look back, reflect, and celebrate our growth and successes.

When you meet each month, you will re-read and revise the original list of traits that attracted you to your partner. This is a wonderful opportunity to have honest conversations about the elements that may be lacking in the relationship. For example, if one person loved how much the other person liked to travel, and this person no longer has that interest, it would make sense that aspects of the relationship deteriorate. This is why honesty is the most important (and challenging) element of the contract. It is crucial that you are completely transparent about your satisfaction level in the relationship, each month. This is the chance to affirm your partner in all the ways they are showing up for you, in the way your needs are met, and to offer them feedback on what would make you feel more seen, and more connected.

The purpose of approaching your relationship as a contractual agreement is the understanding that a contract is void unless its terms and conditions are met.

It is possible that, as you navigate the monthly check-ins with your partner, you begin to notice that certain fundamental needs are not being addressed in the way you need them to be. In fact, it is possible that you notice how all the patterns you have been hoping will change, aren't changing. If you find yourself in this position, you will inevitably face a question: will or won't you continue to stay in a relationship that does not satisfy you? The purpose of the contractual relationship is to give you the tools and space to create the most fulfilling relationship possible. If you find that the contract is not meeting your fundamental needs, you and your partner may agree to part ways. We don't believe that a relationship is successful simply because it lasts. We believe that a successful relationship is a truthful relationship. And sometimes the most honest thing you can do is say: "you know what, this is no longer working for me." If by the end of this book you decide that you no longer want to be in the relationship you came to these pages with, we will also consider that to be a success. The reason for this is that we consider success to be living your truth out loud, whatever your truth may be.

A NOTE FOR OUR READER

Who you are: we have written this book for people interested in challenging the paradigm through which you approach your relationship with your partner and your relationship with yourself.

What we offer: *The Relationship Contract* is a guide you can follow with prompts designed to deepen your communication.

The nature of communication–how, when, and why we talk–is what distinguishes a mediocre relationship from one in which you feel seen and heard. Through The Relationship Contract we will guide you along a series of questions and exercises you can use as departing points for the most important tool in the handbook: the commitment to find your chairs every month and discuss the status of your relationship.

A Disclaimer: The Relationship Contract is not a substitute for couple's counseling, or for individual therapy. The presence of a licensed third party is invaluable in pointing each person toward the work they need to do as individuals, as well as solidifying the work you end up doing as a couple. On page 25 you will find an interview we conducted with therapist Sarah Barrett Lepore, to provide a therapist's insight into the communication hurdles a couple can face.

Research shows that the way we show up to our partners is formulated around our experiences as children, within family systems. Specifically, conflict and conflict avoidance methods are directly and indirectly passed down through generations. As you make your way through this handbook, we invite you to reflect on the specific wounds you might be carrying that could be influencing the way you feel about your partner. This handbook is not intended to address those wounds (that is what the excellent therapists are for), instead, it is a tool designed to help you and your partner identify those wounds and create the space to show them to one another, so that you may be better understood.

In order to correct a pattern that does not work, first you have to name it. This is where "Finding Your Chairs" every month becomes especially useful, and your honesty is paramount. At first, this may be difficult, but you have to let yourself believe that no preference is too small: this is the time for you to tell your partner what you really need, and what is really bothering you.

An article went viral a few years ago, in which a man wrote about how his wife left him because he left an empty glass beside the sink, every night. The empty glass became a symbol of the man's lack of regard for his wife's requests. It was also a symbol for the unwanted role this woman occupied: as a care-taker, not a partner. What is sad about this story is that, on some level, it doesn't matter what you do to please your partner if you aren't doing the specific things they cherish. This man could bring her all the flowers in the world, and still, all she wanted was a glass-less sink.

We often delude ourselves into thinking that we are doing so much for each other, but we don't take the time to determine whether our actions are having the impact we intend. We wonder: if this couple had been in counseling, if they'd found their chairs every month, if they had worked their relationship contract, would they still be married? At the very least, the empty glass by the sink would have come up, every month, again and again, until it was resolved.

Our hope is that The Relationship Contract and the monthly meetings within them will provide couples the opportunity to talk about the small things, like the empty glasses, before the small things build up to big, insurmountable things.

And: it is entirely possible that, through these meetings, it becomes clear that the small things aren't correctible: that they represent a deeper incompatibility. In this case, we also want to offer you tools to support you through a separation. You will find specific resources for divorce and separation, toward the end of this book.

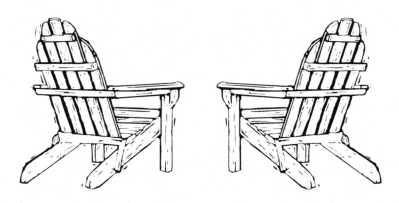

FINDING YOUR CHAIRS

(COMMUNICATION)

Most days, at sunrise and at sunset, we sit together for five or ten minutes, as it creates an important point of contact. We use this time to meditate and chat about our upcoming plans. Sometimes, when one of us needs to talk about or clarify something, we will say let's "Find our Chairs". There may be times when one of us won't quite be in the space in which we can sit down and listen, which is completely understandable. In this case, we will say something like: "can we find our chairs in an hour or maybe tomorrow?" The purpose of 'Finding our Chairs" is to do so only when we feel emotionally available to be present.

We suggest you try this. For one week, experiment with setting a time, choosing your chairs, and telling your partner what they can do to support you. The key element of this exercise is that it forces us to take accountability and communicate to our partner what we might need.

It can also be a wonderful time to express gratitude for the ways they have supported you so far. And, don't forget to ask the golden question when you find your chairs: *what can I do to make you feel loved today?*

When we spoke to a young, newly married couple, they shared their routine of asking each other each morning over coffee, "How's the weather up there"? This was their way of asking each other to express their feelings for the day. If it was "cloudy or stormy or sunny" that gave the partner a clear picture of the support needed. We felt that this was extremely insightful.

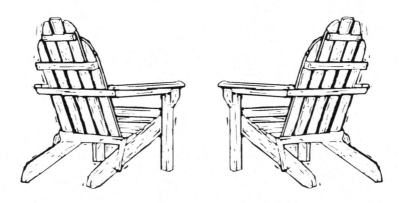

BEING COMFORTED IS MORE IMPORTANT THAN BEING COMFORTABLE

(CONNECTION)

The difference between authentic connection and comfortable compatibility is subtle, but meaningful. Being comfortable in someone's presence is not the same thing as being comforted by someone's presence. Being listened to is not the same thing as being heard. If you are asking yourself whether you have chosen your relationship out of comfort, or out of connection, ask yourself this: when I am with this person, am I being my most authentic self? Also ask yourself this: how does my nervous system feel when I am in the presence of my partner?

It's important to pay attention to the ways our bodies can indicate discomfort. One of the elements we most appreciate about our relationship is the way we feel fundamentally safe and at ease in each other's presence. This safety is anchored in a simple belief: neither of us believe that the other would ever do anything to intentionally hurt each other.

This understanding allows us to approach conversations with creativity. Even if we disagree about something, we trust that we are going to be able to reach resolution with compassion. It is always us against the problem, not us against each other. In other words: we never interact with each other as if the other person is the problem.

Some signs that might indicate you feel unsafe or are hiding your authentic self include: censoring your needs, withholding information, and being used to feeling unseen. You might even think to yourself, "I don't like the person I am in this relationship."

If you've been together for a month, or a year, or three years, or six, and deep down you truly believe your relationship isn't right, it is important that you end it as gracefully as possible (toward the end of this handbook, we have compiled a list of resources for this, too). The longer you stay in a dissatisfying relationship, the worse your outlook on life will become, and the worse your outlook on life becomes, the more you will act against your own best interests.

This is where the contractual relationship becomes especially useful, and the monthly practice of "Finding Your Chairs" is essential. These are the opportunities for you to evaluate the nature and strength of your connection, bearing in mind that, if the contract isn't working, you have the freedom to end it at any time.

A deep connection requires you to see, and be seen, fully and authentically. You are the only person who can determine what you need, to feel seen. Some questions to ask yourself might be: when do I feel most at ease? When do I feel most relaxed? What are the common ingredients in the best days of my life?

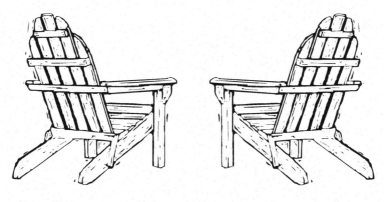

LISTEN TO YOURSELF COMPLETELY

(COMPASSION)

The emotional body and the logical mind are often one in the same. The way we feel informs our thoughts, and our thoughts inform the way we feel. Philosopher Anaïs Nin writes: "We don't see things as they are; we see things as we are." This feedback loop is essentially human. The ability to recognize the loop in ourselves and in others is what separates an active relationship from a reactive relationship. In action, there is the space to respond with presence, compassion, and intuition. In reaction, we become victims to our egos, to our minds, and to our emotions.

One of the most compassionate acts we can do, as humans, is to learn how to articulate our physical and emotional needs and preferences to ourselves, and to our partners. This sounds simple and straightforward, but it requires that we do something we often run away from, which is: to listen to ourselves completely, and with love.

Listening to ourselves can be as subtle as noticing that we have a small headache, or that we are thirsty. This perception may seem insignificant, but in reality, a headache will change the way we carry ourselves, the way we speak to our partners. The tone of our voice can become heavy with impatience, when, in reality, we're just in pain. In this case, communicating the reality of a physical experience presents the opportunity for your partner to support you--for example, by offering you a tylenol and a glass of water.

All truths, no matter how minor, deserve to be expressed freely and fluidly. This freedom of expression is the foundation on which deep trust is built.

A moment in which Dan demonstrated significant compassion toward me is when I lost my beloved dog, Sam, my companion of seventeen years. The death of a pet creates an extraordinary abyss within, alleviated only through patience and compassion. As I mourned, Dan held space for me to grieve. This looked like sitting with me quietly, offering small distractions (like laughter), and listening to me talk when I felt up to it. His compassion is what allowed me to grieve my loss fully, without having to minimize or rush the process. In turn, this deepened the trust in the relationship, as it proved I could show up to Dan however I felt, and that I would be safe, loved, and heard.

When I asked Dan to reflect and share a moment in which I demonstrated significant compassion toward him, he also spoke of a moment of loss: the death of his brother. Sometimes Dan needed to talk, sometimes he needed space to be with his thoughts. My intention through his grieving process was to be a steady constant presence that reassured him that he was taken care of, seen, heard, loved. This is what we seek when we find ourselves at grief's doorstep: someone to hold our hand and walk us through the doorway, so we can experience the breadth and depth of our emotions, and begin the process of healing and reflecting.

Sometimes we do things we think our partner needs because we are the ones who need them. So, rather than guess what your partner might need during an extenuating time, we recommend that you ask this question: **what is the best way for me to show you how loved you are, in this moment?** The answer will vary according to the person and where they are in their grief process. The key is to remove guessing from the equation, to the best of our capacity. The most present thing we can do in the throes of life's hurdles is to listen, deeply, with attention and with care.

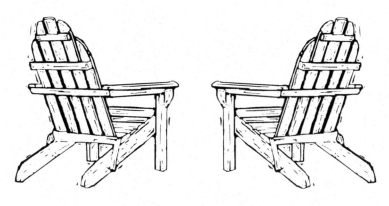

THE MOST IMPORTANT RESOURCE

(TIME)

Every morning and every night we find our chairs and sit together for a few minutes (or hours). We'll have a cup of coffee or a glass of wine, and talk about our days. Sometimes, we'll use this time to process and unpack something one of us has been thinking about (for example, an upcoming family gathering, a situation at work, an idea for a creative project.) "Finding our Chairs" is what we most look forward to each day–it is a sacred block of time that allows us the space to be with one another and connect, sometimes silently, but always intentionally.

We believe our relationship to time is deeply dictated by our relationship to mortality. Writer Annie Dillard says: "how you spend your days is how you spend your life." Because of this, it is crucial to understand you and your partner's relationship with time, and how you each want to spend it. Not everyone has the space or availability to start and end their days together–perhaps you're the kind of person who prefers to unwind alone at the end of the day, or maybe you'd rather go on a walk with your partner rather than sitting still. There is no right answer, there is just the right intention—the philosophy behind "finding your chairs" is to find a way to meaningfully spend time together, even if there are no chairs involved.

As you read this chapter, we invite you to consider your relationship with time. How do you most enjoy spending it? What do you like to do alone? What do you like to do with your partner? Do you prefer to go to the grocery store by yourself, or do you enjoy having company? Do you like to arrive places early? Are you comfortable running a few minutes late? Did you grow up in a household where punctuality was respected, or was it eschewed?

Take a few moments to write down your answers. Then ask yourself: in which ways is my life aligned with the ways I enjoy spending time? And in which ways is it not?

Once you have reflected on this for yourself, we invite you to explore these same questions with your partner. Find out what time means to them, how they like to spend it, how they do not like to spend it. Keep in mind that many factors will influence the way a person is socially conditioned and allowed to interact with time. For example: in professional settings, research data and studies prove that women who are not punctual experience more disciplinary action than men. These social conditions, while seemingly imperceptible in a day to day relationship, are powerful factors that predict how someone will interact with time, which affects the way they will plan and approach day-to-day life.

Talking about and understanding time is important because planning and logistics are crucial elements in any long-term relationship. The more responsibilities the relationship has, for example: children, grand-children, businesses, mutual hobbies, the more planning and logistical conversations will be required. All these conversations will demand a common ground and fluency with time: how much there is, and how to spend it.

Early on in our relationship we spoke about our relationship to time. I have a background in paramedics, and Dan used to be in the military. We understand that the sound of a siren means someone's life has irrevocably changed, and that minutes can mean the difference between life and death.

One day, as Dan drove down the highway, he saw a car flip. Without pausing to think, he stopped, pulled the driver from the leaking car, and dragged her to safety. It wasn't until an hour later that he realized he was covered in tears and blood. In the same way that my medical background trained me to act before I thought or felt, Dan's military background also trained him to react quickly. It is important for us both to hold our specific backgrounds in mind, as they dictate both our present reactions as well as our overarching relationship to time. We understand that anything can change in a matter of seconds, which makes our daily time in our chairs a sacred space of connection and devotion.

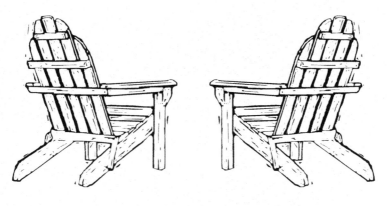

HOW LONG DO YOU WANT TO LIVE HERE?

(LIMITING THOUGHTS)

The way we interact with our reality is dictated by the thoughts we train ourselves to think. The National Science Foundation estimates that humans process approximately 50,000 thoughts a day. It is interesting to think about the nature of these thoughts: how many of them are habitual, how many of them serve us, and how many of them work against us. Most of us experience limiting thoughts on an hourly basis. A limiting thought can sound like: *"I am not good enough," "My partner won't understand," "I can't."* In other words: a limiting thought always contains an element of scarcity, as well as the fear that we won't be able to overcome this scarcity. However, in the same way that we can train our body to adjust to a new diet or a new sleep schedule, we can also reprogram the neural pathways in our brain that reinforce limiting thoughts. First, it is important to be aware of what these thoughts are.

We recommend that you start with a simple exercise: make a list of the limiting thoughts you catch yourself thinking every day. Pay attention to the thoughts that create a constricting feeling in your chest. Examples can include:

I am afraid of:

I am worried that:

I am nervous about:

This won't work out because:

Once you are aware of the limiting thoughts, make a list of thoughts that counter the limiting narrative. Examples can include:

I am capable of:

I am hopeful because:

I feel relieved that:

I will succeed because:

Once you have both lists, we invite you to compare and contrast the belief systems of the limited thoughts against the belief systems of the empowered thoughts. You will notice that empowered thoughts all share a core belief, which is the understanding that you happen to your life, as opposed to the idea that life happens to you. Similarly, you will notice that the empowered thoughts have a way of settling and relaxing your nervous system. Conversely, limited thoughts are physically uncomfortable: they always create a universe in which you do not have agency. They usually sound like the voice of someone who does not believe in you: *you can't, it's too hard, it's impossible.*

Once you are aware of the limiting thoughts that affect your day-to-day living, you will also notice the way these thoughts influence and dictate the way you show up in your intimate relationships. If we are in the practice of limiting ourselves, we will inadvertently limit our partner or expect our partner to limit themselves on our behalf. At first, this might look small: one person might get an exciting opportunity and the other person might ask: "are you sure you can handle all that responsibility?", rather than encouraging them.

The problem with this response is that it is coming from a limited perspective, and it promotes self-doubt and limitation. Another example is how one person might stop socializing and going out with friends in order to make their partner more comfortable. Self-imposed limitations and sacrifices of this nature set the stage for resentment, and also establish the expectation that the other person will make similar sacrifices, when the time comes. If your relationship is based on the structure of limitation and scarcity, you will eventually limit and be limited in your long-term relationship. This in turn will affect the way you see and interact with the world, which perpetuates the vicious cycle of self-imposed limitation.

SO, WHAT DO WE DO WHEN WE CATCH OURSELVES IN LIMITATION?

First, it is important to acknowledge there are many reasons our minds are conditioned to impose limitations. Each of us come from a unique history: we may have experienced family trauma, oppression, marginalization, disenfranchisement, etc. It can be as automatic as breathing to perpetuate the cycle of limitation without being aware you are doing it. A question to ask yourself is: what need is being served when I limit myself? We believe that the reason people limit themselves is because, on some level, they are afraid of the responsibility it takes to live a life without limitation.

For example: if you tell yourself you are not good enough to get a promotion, you are avoiding having to do the work or taking the responsibility it would require for you to be good enough for the promotion. If you tell yourself you'll never be able to write a book, you are avoiding sitting in front of the blank page and generating the words required for a book. Likewise, if you tell your partner that you don't want them to go out whenever they want, you are avoiding whatever you would learn from being alone for a few hours. **It is easy to become used to the idea we have of ourselves or another, instead of putting in the work it takes to consistently observe each nuanced stage of evolution.**

Once again: the opposite of limitation is empowerment. Empowerment is the intentional practice of gratitude for everything that is working. Empowerment is the intention to get through life's expected turbulence without causing unneeded turbulence. To hold oneself with empowerment is not blind optimism: it is the practice of understanding and assessing where and how you can have the most impact, and where it is best for you to surrender.

SO, NEXT TIME YOU CATCH YOURSELF IN A SPIRAL OF LIMITATION: ASK YOURSELF..... HOW LONG DO I WANT TO LIVE HERE?

This question has several functions. First, it brings awareness to the fact that you are experiencing the effects of limited thinking. Second, it shows you that you are choosing what to do with your mind. In the same way you are choosing to exist in limitation, you could conversely choose to exist in empowerment. Lastly, this question reminds you that you can decide how long you want to stay in anxiety, or fear. The more careful, compassionate, and disciplined we are in our thinking, in our own individual lives, the better we can show up for our partners and for our communities at large.

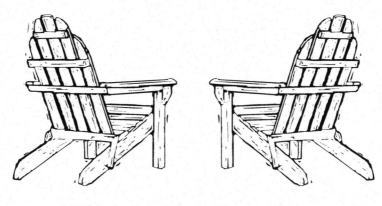

ASK YOUR BODY NOT YOUR BRAIN

(IN CONVERSATION WITH A THERAPIST)

As we mentioned earlier, the relationship contract is not a substitute for the kind of healing that can happen through counseling or therapy. Most people believe that couples who end up in counseling are "past the point of no return" so to speak, that they have developed problems so deep only a mediator can solve them. This couldn't be further from the truth. In fact, if you have the time and resources, we recommend that you and your partner meet with a therapist, even if you've never had a fight, even if you've only been together for a few months. Counseling has the capacity to reveal the patterns we bring to our intimate relationships, patterns that are usually formulated within our early relationships with our nuclear family. Throughout the next pages you will read an interview we conducted with a therapist we trust and admire, to provide a sense of the insight you might glean through therapy.

Sarah Barrett Lepore started her career path intuitively at 17 years old when she chose to treat her depression and anxiety by using physical exercise, music and nutrition. The way the body could change the mind's perspective in an instant was fascinating to her, and the fields of Health and Psychology quickly became her two passions. She attended college, got bachelor degrees in both fields and went on to get a Master's Degree from Naropa University in 1999. In this experience-based graduate program she learned first hand the effects of meditation and mindfulness on the brain, traditional cognitive/ behavioral therapy and deeper therapies such as bodymind psychotherapy, energy healing and transpersonal counseling techniques.

So in your opinion Sarah: what makes a healthy relationship?

Interdependence, vulnerability, chemistry/attraction, and laughter. An authentic desire to give and receive love solely from one another, free of ulterior motives like money, family expectations, cultural expectations, etc. You don't want to be enmeshed: you have to stand on your own two feet. Or if the only thing you do together is a sport and one of you breaks your leg, or gets arthritis etc., then what happens? There is a lot of self work to do whether we are in a relationship or not. The most important relationship is the one with ourselves.

What is the difference between the healing/work the individual is responsible for, as opposed to the healing/work the couple is responsible for?

Happiness is an inside job. If one is depressed it's their job to seek professional help on their own. Of course, a partner can notice and encourage the need for help without disdain or blame. When we can have a healthy relationship with oneself and have physical, mental, emotional respect for the other, then larger issues between couples need not exist. Self responsibility and genuine care as well as respect for the other, equals a foundation for a happy relationship

WHAT ARE SOME CORE ISSUES YOU NOTICE PEOPLE/COUPLES RUN INTO IN THEIR RELATIONSHIPS?

1. Lack of self worth. When one is dependent on the other for worthiness it can breed jealousy. Enmeshment causes this too.

2. Trauma looping aka early attachment disruption getting played out unconsciously in the current timeline.

3. Focus of control - underlying beliefs that one can make the other happy if they do x, y, z and in those actions they are compromising their own truth.

From what you have observed, what are the most effective tools of communication?

Methods of communication that involve bringing what's unconscious to the conscious mind. This requires diligent work to notice emotional triggers. For example, to take a pause, a breath, a choice to respond rather than react out of old habits. It is important to build an inner witness/co-consciousness on one's own in order to take personal responsibility for what and how you communicate your feelings to your partner. It takes effort and work, and humility.

How does an individual become aware of the pain/traumas they are bringing into a relationship?

In my work when someone presents a complaint in their relationship dynamic I always inquire if this is a familiar issue for them and if so how early they remember having this issue in their lives. This can begin to remind the client that they have learned this behavior from a survival drive i.e. hide, avoid, submit, fight, flight, freeze, collapse, and that reaction is no longer needed in their adult relationships. Then it goes back to self awareness, noticing the defense/trigger, pausing and taking care of oneself before making a permanent decision in a temporary state of mind. We work to repair old trauma, loops, and create new healthy attachments and patterns.

When should someone walk away from a relationship they are invested in?

My contention is that no one can tell someone to leave: it needs to come from within the relationship. However, generally when efforts are made by both parties for a significant amount of time with no change and growth it becomes important to discuss the reality of happiness being attained by staying together. Everyone has their own meter for how much they can give or take, how much they love and adore the other, etc. People grow at different rates, and people have different levels of patience with the growth process based on how much they respect and care and love their partner. There is no specific time. It is completely up to the person's intuition and how much they want to work on it. Sometimes people spend their lives settling because they don't want to go through the pain of unraveling lives. No one can tell anyone else that it is time to separate. It has to come from you, even though it can certainly help to have an external witness.

How do you listen to your intuition? How does that practice become cultivated?

I work with people often on this. A phrase I use a lot is "ask your body not your brain and say the first thing that comes." A lot of the time, people who have had trauma in childhood (which is basically everybody) are blocked from their intuition. We are told: don't see this, don't do that, don't act on that. Children are meant to be seen and not heard. We have to cut ourselves off of our intuition to survive. Then we grow up: we change what we do to get love. There is this idea of: "I cannot share my truth because it will hurt the other person." So, I will change who I am to be who they want me to be because I need love so badly. This is what we do to survive, but there is always a paradox. It is scary to be in your truth and to be vulnerable. So, to help people connect back to their voice is a repair job. It is a lot of coming back to your body, checking in on that energy, on the frequency and vibrations. It is restoring the connection to our bodies that our culture has severed. You have to use every angle in order to heal. Disease is also emotional and spiritual and it can help the physical body when you address it at those levels. Some people don't even notice when they are breathing. So a lot of my work is an invitation for people to just begin to notice their bodies. If you do this, you can make decisions from an informed place, both within yourself and in your relationship.

Sometimes our partner may not value the importance of communication. How do you explain the importance of communication?

My contention is that it's not the job of the partner to teach this, as it can create a power differentiation. You're in this together. If one party notices that their issue with communication is affecting the marriage, it is their responsibility to learn how to communicate better. If they don't want to, I say, NEXT!

In your opinion, how often do people change?

Honestly, it's rare in what I see. It can take years. There are so many layers of pain that culminates into what a person is and who they become as an adult. It takes bravery. The emotional world ends up affecting the physical world. We are unwell if we avoid and push away. People can only do that for so long. It is really a matter of if they are willing to take the reins and look at themselves. Even going to get therapy is an old mentality of believing the therapist should fix the patient. I assign practice, things to do to help yourself, and if we don't have a good relationship with ourselves we won't have a good relationship with anyone. You have to have respect for yourself in order to have respect for others.

What exercises can couples use in bettering their communication?

Play games, have new experiences together, get out of old habits and try new routines. Use first person statements to explain energy exchanges, "my gut feels butterflies" "my palms are sweaty" "I'm nervous and I can tell because I'm shaking" "I'm afraid of doing or saying something wrong." These can be openers for people to allow the other party to build empathy for the honesty that's being expressed. It also helps to do things side by side rather than face to face, as it is less threatening. Going on road trips, amusement parks, taking a walk, sitting on a park bench... experiment to break up the rigidity of old patterns. SLOW IS FAST. Take your time. When one is afraid of communicating it is typically rooted in childhood shame and requires lots of room, patience, kindness and understanding for the partner to hold room for the one afraid to step into this new way of being.

What is intimacy?

Vulnerability in connection with another. Being your true self and being loved and offering love from a place of compassion for others, and not from neediness, and accepted for that.

How often do you think nuclear families make relationships harder and what can one do to make that easier?

Nuclear families bring in trauma from lineages way before them. Looking at this requires personal responsibility, stopping the finger pointing victim/persecutor/rescuer drama triangle, and releasing judgment. Learning how to become curious about the patterns being played out so there can be room to take a pause in the heat of the moment and make the choice to step toward love, rather than defense against the other. Underneath all the drama people crave love and connection.

Why are people afraid of being alone?

Being alone is an illusion. We are never really alone. As long as there is an ocean or a tree, there is a life force that exists around us and in us. If we can breathe we are not alone.

MOVE YOUR FEET

(THE WHEEL OF PURPOSE)

The first and most important relationship you must tend to is the one you have with yourself. If you do not know yourself, if you do not have a sense of your daily needs and wants, you will tacitly and unconsciously expect your partner to fulfill needs they are not responsible for. This is why the following tool, "The Wheel of Purpose," is foundational to the relationship contract.

Two years ago Dan developed the "Wheel of Purpose." This project would go on to change his life, and set the tone for his future relationship with me.

The philosophy of the wheel boils down to the idea that integration is essential to a well-balanced life. Integration, in this case, involves paying close attention to six areas: physical health, mental health, spirituality, work, play, and relationships. Individually, each area strengthens the overall quality of your life. When worked on and practiced in unison, each area feeds and enhances another.

The idea is for both partners to keep each other accountable to their individual wheels of purpose, and to the shared wheel they create together as a couple. The wheel of each relationship becomes the shared set of values a couple holds, and is completely individual and subjective. It is also something that can change over time: what you value now might not be what you value later.

With this in mind, these are the six parts of the wheel of purpose:

RELATIONSHIPS:

The relational area of your life holds a vast amount of opportunity. Many of us struggle to allow ourselves to be seen and present with one another. When we pay attention to the relationships in our lives, it means we are asking ourselves critical questions, such as: how do I feel in my relationship with my parents/friends/coworkers? Do I have people in my life I can talk to, about everything? In which ways do I learn from the people around me?

Studies show that it doesn't really matter whether we have two friends or twelve; what matters is that we move around the world feeling supported by our chosen community. This takes time, energy, and generosity, as relationships are usually often the first thing you'll sacrifice to make room for whatever else you perceive as important—career, self, personal projects, etc.

However, at the end of the day, life comes down to the quality of your relationships. So: do you have engaging friendships? A personal connection with the people you work with? How is your marriage? How is your marriage *really*?

Almost every relationship can be improved with a simple conversation. Here, we will offer you some tools and stories to give you ideas on how to re-connect with people that are important to you and to re-discover people you love.

PHYSICAL HEALTH:

Everyone has different bodies with different preferences and needs. What is undeniable, however, is the connection between physical well-being and emotional well-being. The "physical health" area of the wheel is specifically dedicated to carving time for you to work on your health, in any way you need. This might look like cooking with more vegetables every week, or taking bike rides, or starting a morning yoga practice, or simply drinking more water. Keep in mind that every step, however small, is a movement in the direction of your well-being. This in itself will support you in every other area of your life. You can't change your mindset without changing your behaviors and you can't change your behaviors unless you are willing to make changes to your life.

My longstanding interest in physical health motivated me to build a business of fitness studios. Dan's long standing entrepreneurship motivated him to work with me to open the studios.

The reason we include this story is because: you never know where one section of the wheel will lead you. It is possible that you will find that what you thought was a hobby (fitness) in fact becomes a profession. You may also find that as you dedicate time to practicing physical health, all kinds of space opens up in your heart and mind to make new strides, in new directions.

PLAY:

The beautiful thing about play is that only you can define what it means to you: games, sports, socializing, reading. To carve out time for play is to allow space for the child-like part of ourselves to exist out in the world. Without that space and play, we'll do what all children do when they are fussy and bored: we'll throw a tantrum, often directed at the people closest to us.

There's a story we like to tell, about a man (let's call him Bob) who was tired of his every-day life. His job was boring, his marriage was flat, and he felt exhausted all the time. Eventually, he decided to pick up bowling because he remembered that it made him happy in high-school. For Bob, bowling was play. The physical workout gave him more energy, he was happier, he joined a bowling league, made friends, his wife joined too, and the marriage got its spark back. That's the thing about play: it's key to everything else.

It is as crucial to play with your partner as it is to find what play means to you, as an individual. Couples that practice joy routinely infuse their days with opportunities to connect, laugh, and enjoy. One of the things we knew for sure is that we were looking for a partner with whom we could play. For us, this means late nights spent listening to music, drinking wine, playing pool, or cards, or chess. It means dancing by the swimming pool and grilling a late-night meal.

WORK:

For many of us, our work occupies the majority of both our conscious and unconscious minds. If we are not at work, we are thinking about work. The more successful we become, the more this happens. Work is how we earn money and consumes a massive part of how we spend our time. It is important then to be in a constant dialogue with this area of our life, so that we can learn to make conscious and present choices about our work, rather than let fear drive our professional lives.

Some questions to ask yourself, as you contemplate this section of this wheel is: to what degree has fear informed your professional choices? If scarcity were not an issue, which field would you be in?

As we mentioned above, one of the foundational elements that brought us together was our shared professional vision. In order to execute this vision, we had to have a series of honest conversations in which we expressed our goals, hopes, and dreams. From previous experience, we know how difficult it can be to articulate desires and ambitions to partners who may not share them (or may not be emotionally available to share them.) If this is true for you, we ask you the same question Dan asked me in the beginning:

If you had a magic wand you could wave and instantly change your life, what would you change?

SPIRITUALITY:

We hold a rigorous spiritual practice, as individuals and as a couple. We begin each morning with meditation, and we follow *A Course of Miracles*. For us, grounding ourselves in our spirit is a fundamentally important part of our lives.

When we use the word "spirit" we mean faith, hope, God, joy--any body of knowledge or belief system that inspires you to be a more integrated person. Whether this looks like strict religious observation, or a daily affirmation, is each individual's sacred choice to make. This area of the wheel is the time alone you spend in dialogue with your higher self. It is the space where you learn how to be a more grounded, centered, and generous person. The time we dedicate to spirit is special because it is the only time specifically devoted to something beyond the tangible world, as in, the only time we dedicate ourselves to humbly understanding there is always something we don't know.

We refer to Spirit as "God's Plan", which may or may not look like we think it should. We have found that understanding that God may have a different plan allows us to be open to shifts we may not be able to explain. Numerous times we have looked back and realized there was a reason for a delay, or change, and it was for the better. Sometimes God has a better plan.

EMOTIONAL HEALTH:

This final part of the wheel is the one we are going to dedicate the least time and space to, specifically because a wealth of books and information exists, assembled by experts, therapists, doctors, and professionals in the field. There are experiences we as humans undergo--the loss of a parent, illness, depression, marital problems, addictions--that will not be healed with a good marriage, or a workout routine, or a spiritual practice, or many friends. There are problems and wounds only therapists and doctors have the breadth and resources to treat. One of the most singular and transformative gifts we can give to those around us is the pursuit of healing, sometimes in the form of therapy. Traditional therapy is something every single person can benefit from powerfully. At the end of this book, you will find a list of resources we have curated, with people who have devoted their whole lives and careers to healing. Additionally, there are many forms of healing that aren't found within therapeutic contexts. This can look like group meetings with our peers, volunteering, spending time with people we trust on a cellular level.

Fundamentally, we cannot be good partners if we aren't capable of being responsible for ourselves, first. One of the most loving acts we can do for ourselves (which extends to our partners) is to address any issues that might hamper our ability to connect with our partner in a meaningful way. In order to do this, one must first take inventory of one's emotional health, which can be an extraordinarily daunting thing to do if you are not in the habitual practice of asking yourself: how am I feeling today?

In order to begin to have this relationship with yourself, we suggest that you start taking note of how you feel, day-to-day. You can make a note in your phone or in a journal, and it can be as simple as assigning a numeric value to your mood. Using the scale of 1-10, 1 would be "terrible/in a critical place," whereas 10 might be "fantastic." This method can be useful: the moment you begin to notice too many low numbers for too many days in a row, it is a clear indicator that you are in need of external support.

HOW TO APPLY THE WHEEL

We suggest that you integrate the wheel of purpose into your monthly meetings, when you and your partners find your chairs. In the same way that you hold each other accountable to the lists you write every month, we encourage you to ask each other questions:

How is your wheel going?

Which part of the wheel did you devote most time to this month?

Which part did you devote least time to?

Which part will be especially important to you this month, and what can I do to support that?

From these questions, you can derive actionable items that will guide you on how to help your partner care for themselves in the way they most need. And: you can ask for the specific things that you will need to tend to the part of the wheel you find most important, at that time.

The beauty of the wheel is that once you start working on one area, you will notice how its positive effects impact every area. Spiritual health is directly linked to emotional health, which increases the quality of relationships, and so on. To get started, we invite you to select a specific section of the wheel and dedicate a full week to it. Or, if that feels overwhelming, you can identify a small action you could take within each section of the wheel (taking a walk, calling a friend, a therapist, reaching out to a professional contact, praying, playing a game of chess), and focus on that, too.

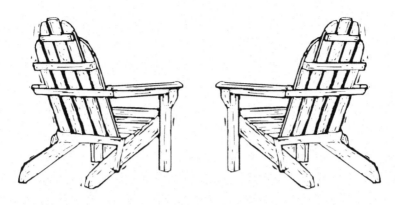

THE PARTS OF US WE BELIEVE ARE THE HARDEST TO LOVE ARE THE MOST IMPORTANT PARTS TO EXPRESS

(PARTNERSHIP)

Relationship expert Esther Perel writes about the Four Horsemen, by John Gottman, that signify the demise of a relationship: criticism, contempt, stonewalling, and defensiveness. It is interesting to observe how these four horsemen play off one another: the person who feels criticized will act defensive. The person who experiences the stonewalling will often feel contempt for the person doing the stonewalling. Esther Perel also writes about how each of these horsemen is associated with a primal unmet need: people do not behave dysfunctionally on purpose. Rather, people often have dysfunctional behavior modeled for them, which they replicate unconsciously. If criticism, contempt, stonewalling, and defensiveness are the four horsemen that warn us of the apocalypse, what are a relationship's guardian angels?

The opposite of criticism is affirmation. The opposite of contempt is respect. The opposite of stonewalling is to invite. The opposite of defensiveness is openness. To affirm someone is to make them feel seen and validated in their experience. To respect someone is to internally hold them in high regard, and to outwardly communicate that regard. To invite someone into our souls is to allow them to understand us more deeply. To be open is to be available to the truth of who we are, to who our partners are, without the intent to change them or ourselves.

When we treat someone with affirmation and respect, and when we ourselves remain open and invite our partners to know us, we become the guardian angels that protect our relationship.

A beautiful and poignant example of this took place in an experience I shared with Dan.

As a former paramedic, I have seen and experienced accidents on the highway, which makes me quite afraid of cars and the ways they can injure people. In previous relationships I refused to be the passenger, and drove myself and others everywhere. With Dan, I found that I loved the feeling of being driven, of relaxing as he took the wheel. Still, the old trauma in my nervous system would surface in subtle ways, even though I felt safe in the car with Dan.

In order to take care of myself, I articulated my experience of fear to Dan. He started holding my hand as he drove, squeezing tightly to indicate that he was paying close attention to everything that was happening on the road. This small gesture marked the difference between me feeling seen and unseen, safe and unsafe, in a situation outside of my control. Even though neither of us can control the road ahead, we have the capacity to directly influence the feeling and tone of our environment.

All four guardian angels of a relationship are at play in this situation: because I communicated transparently, my feelings have the chance to be affirmed and respected, and Dan can better support me. In another situation, I could continue driving myself everywhere, and never disclose exactly what I needed from Dan in order to feel as safe as possible, and enjoy the feeling of being a passenger. In order to get to this place, I had to overcome the shame I experienced when I realized how afraid of the road I was, even though Dan was a good driver. This is just one small example of the way past pain can influence present behavior.

Every person can relate to experiencing specific forms of shame, and fear. Maybe you were yelled at when you were a kid, so you can't stand loud voices. Maybe you don't like swear-words, and shut down when your partner uses them in your direction. Maybe you hate being touched when you're upset. Whatever it is, most people tend to believe that there is a part of them that makes them hard to love, hard to be with. **One of the foundational elements of the relationship contract, of the monthly meetings, and of finding your chairs every month, is to reinforce the belief that the parts of us we believe are the hardest to love are the most important parts to express, the parts most worthy of affection.**

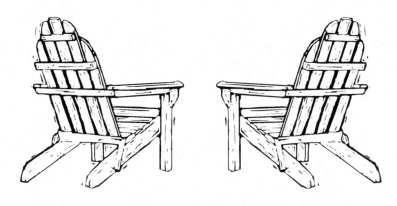

WHEN FALSE EVIDENCE APPEARS REAL

(FEAR)

We like to think of fear as an acronym: FEAR, as in: false evidence appearing real. When we find ourselves in romantic relationships it is easier than ever to act out of fear, out of false evidence appearing real. Previous patterns and wounds can prime us to project intentions onto our partner's behavior, without pausing for a moment to contemplate: is it possible that I am reacting to false evidence appearing real? Is it possible that my partner is tired, hungry, or drained, as opposed to being upset with me?

Here we return to educator Annie Dillard's wonderful quote: how you spend your days is how you spend your life. If you spend your days unaware of the ways you orbit your partner due to your fear, you will spend your life in a constant state of alarm.

Educator and philosopher J. Krishnamurti asks the question: what is the difference between true danger and perceived danger? For example, he writes, when we encounter a rattlesnake in the wild we don't pause to think: we are immediately aware the snake is poisonous, so we flee, or we end up defending ourselves. There is no room for thoughts, no room to judge the snake as "good" or "bad." We simply respond to the danger.

Oftentimes we treat our partners as if they are the rattlesnake, as if they represent the true (as opposed to perceived) danger. It is increasingly easy to fall into this pattern when there is a history of separate trauma, combined trauma, conflict, substance abuse, etc. One of the most difficult and healing milestones in intimate relationships is when both parties understand that there is no rattle-snake, they are not in danger. Once again: the most important belief Dan and I carry is that we would never do anything to intentionally hurt each other. In this context, there is no real danger, there is only safety.

Intimate relationships are the spaces in which we can experiment with the question: what if the only thing to fear is fear itself?

For example, many of us carry a deep fear of rejection and abandonment. This fear can ultimately become projected onto our partners in the form of coercion, because it is easier to attempt to control one's environment than it is to confess how vulnerable we feel. Ultimately, the only way to gracefully move away from fear is to move through it, headfirst. Moving through fear looks like asking uncomfortable questions, having difficult conversations, and being willing to expose parts of ourselves that we hold with shame. Through this sharing, a new relationship becomes possible, in which the goal isn't to eradicate fear, but to give it the opportunity to shift, move, or change.

One of the couples we interviewed as we were putting this book together talked about "little earthquakes," which release pressure from the tectonic plates, thus avoiding the consequences of a larger, devastating earthquake. "Little earthquakes" are the small but important conflicts you will encounter throughout your relationships—opportunities to break through previous patterns, to work through fears.

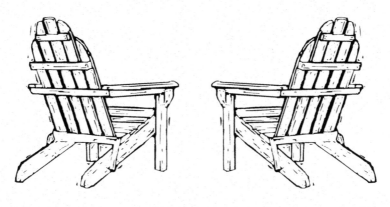

WHAT DOES IT MEAN TO FACE THE FACT OF CHANGE?

(CONTROL)

The most stressful events a human being will go through in their lifetime reportedly include: death, divorce, and moving. What these three scenarios have in common is that they shatter the illusion of control. There is no way to completely prepare for or predict things that are not in our hands. Any relationship that endures time will face moments in which one person or both are not in control. Because of this, one of the most important gifts you can give your partner is to evaluate your personal relationship with control.

Some questions to ask yourself are:

What are the things in your life you have control over?

What are things in life you would like control over?

Conversely, what are the things in your life that you have zero control over?

What is your process as you come to terms with this?

The confusion between what we can and cannot control is one of the greatest sources of suffering any one of us will experience.

This brings us to a separate question: what is your relationship to control in relation to your partner?

Did you enter the relationship hoping you could control/change certain things about them?

Furthermore, did you enter the relationship thinking that *you* might change?

The answer to these questions, for most people who are answering honestly, is yes—we believe our partners will change. Human beings are evolving creatures—in some ways we are always in the process of anticipating our change and the changes of others. Bringing awareness to this tendency can be the difference between natural growth, (positively supporting your partner), and degradation (negatively controlling your partner).

A good example of this comes in the form of substance abuse. If two people enter a relationship at a time when one/both are drinking/partying (this could be due to age/career/lifestyle) it only makes sense to hope/assume that the behavior will change in the future. To think that a person will be exactly the same as they were in their twenties/thirties as they will in their sixties is misguided. However, to assume that the person will do a 180 and change completely is equally misguided.

A question to ask yourself is: what does it mean to face the fact that your partner will change while knowing that you can't control the ways they change?

Secondly: are there ways your partner is changing that are misaligned with your code of values?

And: are there ways that your partner is staying the same that is misaligned with your code of values?

The common element here is that you have to have a clear sense of your code of values in order to engage in a fruitful relationship. You also have to distinguish between your needs and your preferences. Needs are like the main course: if your needs aren't met you'll go hungry. Needs can include: sex, touch, words of affirmation. Preferences are like side dishes: they make the whole meal more interesting and exciting, but you'll still be satisfied without them.

Preferences can include: the temperature of the air conditioning, which side of the bed is slept on, what time to eat dinner. The nature of a preference is that it contains room for compromise, whereas if a need is compromised, the whole relationship can be at risk.

As you conclude this chapter, we encourage you to make a list of preferences and a separate list of needs. A preference might be: "I don't want to sleep with the windows open." A need might be: physical and emotional fidelity. After you have made your lists, find your chairs with your partner, and share them. "Every couple who does this exercise will discover something new about their partner, and about themselves".

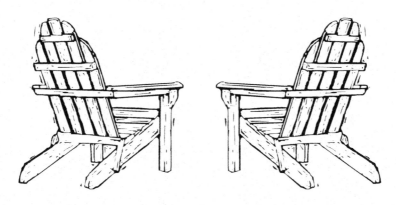

THE MOST IMPORTANT RELATIONSHIP IS WITH YOURSELF

(SPIRITUALITY)

There are specific questions that are important to ask your partner before you commit to a relationship with them. Understanding their relationship to spirituality is crucial. Our understanding of spirituality is simply knowing you are a part of something larger than yourself, and that what you know is limited by your human conditioning.

Spirituality can look like devotion to family, to community service, to a God, to several Gods, to social justice. Spirituality can translate into prayer, service, or action. For example: Dan was raised in a Catholic household, and I was raised by someone who did not believe in a God. Ultimately, we individually and together found our way toward Marianne Williamson's Course of Miracles. This daily practice centers us in our spiritual trajectory, and also creates space for us to engage in deep and meaningful conversation. Our mutual goal is to radically ground ourselves in the present moment, and to move our feet toward inner peace.

One of the most important elements within our partnership is shared devotion. The subject of this devotion depends entirely on the relationship. Some couples are devoted to religion, family, their business, their friends, their community, nature, or animals. It is important that the relationship be about something greater than the individual self. One of the joys of learning and growing as a couple is finding what this is, for each of you.

We are devoted to our daily affirmations. Together and individually, we take time to write 3 times each day. 3-6-9. Three times in the morning, six times in the afternoon, and nine times in the evening. (Dan usually falls asleep early and I have to wake him to write.)

YOU BE YOU

(FREEDOM)

One of the first things Dan and I said to each other when we fell in love was: you be you. What this meant to us was: do anything you need to do to be your most authentic self. It was the opposite of what we had just experienced in our previous relationships.

Many of us gradually leave the parts of us we love behind when we enter a new relationship. Perhaps you loved your solo vacations, your dinner parties with friends, your walks through the park every morning. It is easier to tell yourself that your priorities have changed than it is to stay with the core of who you were before you entered your relationship.

As you read this chapter, we encourage you to write a list of every-thing you value about yourself and the daily habits you engaged in before you entered your relationship. While it is completely normal (and wonderful) to lose some of those habits to the pleasures of new routines and cohabitation, it is important that you continue to carve space for the elements of yourself that you have always loved. In solitude we discover facets of ourselves that are invisible when we are constantly interacting, working, moving, ideating. At the very least, set aside a weekly hour that you spend with yourself, alone, present. You may walk, read, write, draw, or paint, but the most important thing is that the only conversation you have is with yourself. And then, find your chairs with your partner, and share what you have learned with one another.

CAN I TRUST YOU?

(MONEY)

Money is a central reason couples find conflict in relationships: money is tied to a primal sense of survival, and revolves around resources and scarcity. Learning how to communicate about the business of money and its underlying feelings and histories is crucial to build trust, and to execute a shared vision.

Conflicts surrounding money and finances tend to revolve around the greater questions: can I trust you to take care of me/are we going to be okay? So, the first thing to keep in mind is that fighting about money is usually not actually about money. Once again: it comes back down to trust, fear, and scarcity.

People usually fall into one of two categories: they fear abandonment, or engulfment. The people who fear engulfment require space to process and do things on their own. They often perceive control where it doesn't exist, and are reluctant to observe authority. People who fear abandonment are more likely to negate parts of themselves to co-exist in relationships. They would rather change the expectations they have of a situation or a person, than risk upsetting the person by expressing their preferences.

Most people exist along a spectrum between these fears. Most of us, at some point in our lives, may fear both abandonment and engulfment. Understanding where we exist on this spectrum provides important insights as to who we are, and how we communicate.

Many life-altering events are impactful precisely because they cannot be foreseen, and also because we experience our partners in new ways. However, other experiences can be accounted for and anticipated.

One of the most useful things we can do in a relationship, regardless of how long the partnership has been in place, is to create systems to prepare for the unexpected. It is similar to purchasing life insurance or auto insurance: you are dedicating time to ensure the foundation of your relationship can sustain the predictable curveballs life might hurl, which include: death of a family member, assuming large responsibilities, future medical needs, etc.

Dedicating time to these conversations ensures that you have time to discuss and explore elements of you and your partner's personalities that may not have come up in the past. To encounter new emotional terrain as a relationship evolves is inevitable; to be caught completely off guard, however, is preventable.

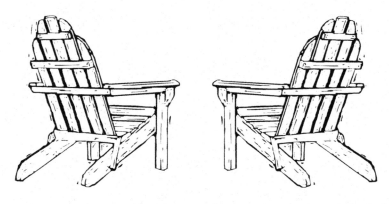

COEXIST
WITHOUT
COMPROMISE

(FAMILY)

It is well documented how children fundamentally alter the quality of the relationships between the parents, both in beautiful and in challenging ways. Children have the capacity to expand and redefine the ways we love: with this emotional expansion also comes stress, fear, and anxiety. Parents often report that the amount of quality time they have with their partners dramatically decreases once they have children. And, the quality time that they do have often turns to discussing the children, which makes sense: children are a big and bright part of our lives.

A question we want to explore with you is: how can you preserve the sacred romantic time between you and your partner, once you have children?

To explore this, we want to address the fact that having children fundamentally alters our nervous system and makes us hypervigilant. Our children depend on us for each and every one of their needs: nourishment, entertainment, security, stimulation, love, attention. For most of us this will translate into a physical attunement and attachment to our child. In other words, we can become wired to gravitate entirely around our children, to the point that it can induce physical anxiety to be away from them. In many aspects this is what it is to be a parent: a big part of our heart now exists outside of our body. However, this constant vigilance can lessen the space and time you have to intimately connect with your partner in contexts that are not about the kids.

In this aspect, it may not be enough to simply set time aside, find your chairs, and have regular date nights. You have to think about what you may need to relax your nervous system so that you can have the inner availability to connect with your partner. This might be that knowing your baby is well-taken care of by someone you trust completely. Or, maybe you need to call and check in on your baby-sitter once every ninety-minutes, to make sure you can be fully present for the duration of the ninety-minutes. Whatever it is, ask yourself: what does my nervous system need in order to disconnect from my vigilant role as a parent, so that I may connect deeply with my partner?

This said, children are not the only cause of hypervigilance in a relationship. Some of us will become the care-takers for our elderly parents, who also require a deep emotional attention as well as our physical presence. Some of us own businesses with employees that depend on us. Some of us are the primary support systems for our friends and family, some of whom might be experiencing struggles we want to help them with.

This leads us to the question: how do we create space for intimacy in our relationships when our responsibilities for others can feel overwhelming?

The first thing we want to offer is advice experts around the world agree on: the first person you need to make time and space for is for yourself. The idea that you would be available to emotionally and intimately engage with your partner while you yourself are saturated, is unrealistic. Before you find your chair with your partner you must first find your chair with yourself. How much time alone do you spend every week? How much time with friends? It can be very easy to turn date-night into yet another item on a list of things to check off, especially if you are already busy. So, first, we invite you to reflect on what making time for yourself might mean for you in particular. Mindful space for yourself is the first step in cultivating the space and time you need for intimacy with your partner.

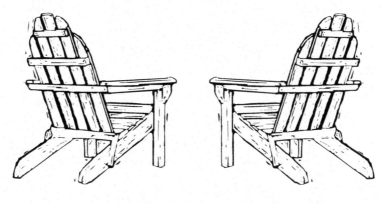

I WOULD NEVER INTENTIONALLY HURT YOU

(CONFLICT)

Every couple has recurring fights: chores, money, children, logistics. The fights themselves can become so habitual each partner assumes a role. The interesting thing about these fights, however, is that they are rarely about what they appear to be on the surface. Arguments about chores are in fact arguments about mutual respect. Arguments about money tend to dredge up feelings of fear and scarcity, etc. One of the most difficult and transformative things a couple can do is learn to quickly identify the deeper conflict underneath the outer disagreement.

The longer people are together the more well-versed and patterned their fights become. Each person eventually assumes a role: the victim, the avoider, the nagger, the apologizer, among others. At a certain point, conflicts, regardless of how minor, become opportunities for each person to re-enact their well-rehearsed role.

A question to ask yourself is: what is my role in conflict, and in which ways am I projecting old patterns onto the way I behave during conflict?

Typically, depending on our upbringing and formative relationships, people respond to conflict in one of four ways: freeze, fawn, fight, flight.

Freezing might look like silence, shutting down, going blank.

Fawning might look like trying to flatter, appease, or otherwise de-escalate a situation in a way that requires the person to ignore how they feel and focus on their partner instead.

Fighting might look like aggression, criticism, confrontation.

Flight ultimately looks like leaving, escaping, withdrawing from a situation all together.

One of the worst mistakes that can happen in a relationship is when people take their partner's responses personally. For example: if someone walks away in the middle of a conflict, it can be tempting to assume that they are doing so in order to be mean, or to make a point, when in reality the person may be experiencing an old response to conflict. Because of this, curiosity becomes the most helpful ingredient we can add to conflict. Rather than ask each other: why are you behaving this way? Instead we must ask: what is the source of this behavior?

A fight about who should do the dishes is not really a fight about dishes: the deeper question tends to be, am I safe with you?

In daily interactions we are constantly asking and answering this question. The need for emotional safety is as basic as the need for food and shelter. In some ways, we are programmed to assess our life-partner in order to determine in which ways they protect us, and in which ways they put us at risk. Risk is to be expected in all intimate relationships: the choice to be vulnerable in itself is a wonderful risk. However, there are also ways in which we can evoke deep feelings in our partner, feelings we may haven't encountered before, which is why it is important to be aware of our responses.

For example: the capacity to recognize when our partner is in a triggered state can mean the difference between an emotionally safe relationship, and one that feels volatile. A triggered state is when the nervous system becomes overwhelmed with stimuli. A triggered person might appear angry and irritated: they are having a physical and psychological response from the past, in the present moment.

Each person exists on a spectrum of how they behave when triggered. Some people experience it lightly, and others really suffer. Being able to have these conversations with your partner openly gives them an opportunity to understand you.

In order to have these conversations, we suggest you find your chairs and start with the following question:

What are some situations that make you feel uncomfortable/afraid, and how can I best support you in those situations? What are things I can do/not do?

Constant fighting is painful and toxic. Conflict, however, can be healthy. Conflict does not look like aggression or a fixation on being "right." Conflict can occur naturally, as two separate organisms require different things to thrive. One person may value a healthy lifestyle, for example, and another might smoke. Depending on the relationship between these two people, this essential difference can either be a point of contention, or conversation. The person who smokes may learn from the person who doesn't, and the person who doesn't smoke may have the opportunity to confront the part of themselves that seeks to help and fix others.

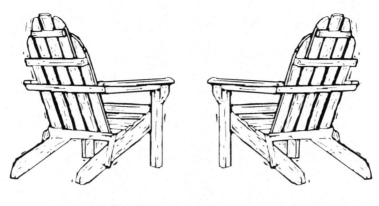

HOW CAN I
MAKE IT BETTER?

(APOLOGIES)

One of the most important communication tools an individual can wield within conflict is the apology. A properly constructed apology is the opportunity to show our partner that we understand how our behavior impacted them. Without this understanding, the behavior will inevitably repeat itself, thus creating a cycle that can become increasingly difficult to break from, as time goes on.

When it comes to conflict it is important to keep in mind that intent and impact are completely different. Even if you would never intentionally hurt your partner you may act in ways that unintentionally create friction. It is normal to become defensive specifically if you never meant to cause harm. However, the faster you can move through the defensiveness to the listening, the sooner you'll begin to understand your partner.

1. **An apology does not include a justification.** If you say the word "but", it is not an apology. If you use the apology as a vehicle to talk about yourself and where you were coming from, it is not

an apology. An apology is only authentic when it creates space for your partner to speak about the impact your actions have had.

2. **The structure of a good apology goes something like this:** "Earlier, when I did [INSERT THING], you indicated that you were upset. I am sorry to have behaved in a way that hurt you. Would you be willing to talk to me more about how you feel?"

3. **An apology is based on accountability.** It demonstrates that you are invested in co-creating a relationship that makes you and your partner feel safe. If you are too busy defending your behavior or blame-shifting to see the areas in which you can improve your communication (you can always improve), then you will miss the opportunity to reflect on the way your behavior impacts others.

4. **The best apology is changed behavior.** Some situations are so severe the only way to move forward is for the behavior to stop completely (for example, if one person struggles with unadulterated rage). However, there is usually more wiggle room with less severe situations that create conflict in relationships. The goal of the apology isn't to obliterate the behavior quickly–it is to bring awareness to it over time. If one person consistently makes another person run behind schedule, for example, a complete apology will ultimately include changed external behavior: alarms, a more clear routine. If the behavior goes unchanged, it is only a matter of time until the consistent friction over "small things" eventually evolves into deep-seated resentment. For this reason, it is incredibly helpful to develop methods to communicate our pet peeves to our partners in low-stakes situations.

The caveat to this chapter is: if you believe you are in a relationship with someone who would intentionally hurt or sabotage you (emotionally, financially, physically), no apology will ever suffice. Their "changed behavior" will only be a manipulation tactic, and staying in the relationship puts you at risk. Some questions to ask yourself, to take the temperature of the relationship, are:

1. Do you often feel as if you are walking on egg-shells around your partner?

2. Do you feel as if you have access to a support system? (Friends, family, co-workers.)

3. Do you feel free to pursue professional/leisure activities that do not include your partner?

4. Do you dress the way you want?

5. Do you feel comfortable expressing and setting boundaries?

6. How does your partner behave when you are in the process of going through "big events" in life? (This could include professional achievements, difficult family situations, moving, depression, etc).

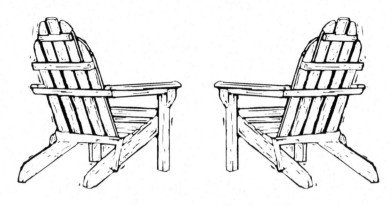

LEAVE THROUGH THE FRONT DOOR, NOT THE BACK DOOR

(DIVORCE)

A key sign that you are in the wrong relationship is if you find yourself compromising your spiritual values in order to appease your partner. It is easier to abandon your principles than it is to demand a deep spiritual interrogation of yourself, and of your partner. This is because you might find that, in order to be true to yourself, you have to leave the relationship. As we mentioned earlier, a relationship that ends because both people understand that they no longer serve each other's higher purpose isn't a failure--it is a success.

It can be extremely difficult to be open and candid about one's feelings, specifically if one is going through a rough patch in one's marriage. There is a tendency to keep the true conflict private, and to present the image of a united front. This, as a practice, is terribly lonely, and leads to a chasmic disconnect between oneself and others. Then, when the divorce or separation inevitably takes place, it appears to have happened out of nowhere—sometimes even to the people who are experiencing it themselves. Even the most sudden occurrences, the most intense catastrophes, are the consequence of a chain of reactions. Nothing ever happens out of nowhere. The key is to recognize the fractures as they happen, and to proceed with the understanding that all relationships fracture in different ways—no one is immune, no matter how resourced or joyous you are. The fractures may come in different forms: financial, medical, relational, familial, but they come. According to relationship experts and therapists, a relationship is only truly in danger when the couple no longer argues—when combustion is replaced with indifference.

This said, the ability to know when to walk away from a relationship has the potential to preserve the integrity of the relationship itself—not just the one between you and your partner, but between you and yourself, and you and your community at large. One of the most traumatic elements of divorce and separation is the rupture that takes place between yourself and the community at large. It's not just losing your partner, it's losing game night with your combined group of friends, or losing the brother in law that has really become a brother.

However, studies show that a high conflict marriage is more physically harmful than divorce. It is possible that, as you navigate the monthly check-ins with your partner, you begin to notice that certain fundamental needs are not getting met. In fact, it is possible that you notice how all the patterns you have been hoping will change, aren't changing. If you find yourself in this position, you will inevitably face a question: will or won't you continue to stay in a relationship that does not satisfy you?

Before we go further, it is important to note the difference between an abusive marriage and a dysfunctional one. An abusive marriage puts one or both partners at physical and emotional risk. A dysfunctional marriage has toxic patterns that erode trust and intimacy, over time. The procedures to leave an abusive marriage are separate and specific.

What we are going to discuss is how to end a marriage that is simply, for whatever reason, not working.

If you are a couple without attachments or assets, the process can be relatively simple.

If you have children and assets, the process becomes more complicated, and your personal history and conflicts with your partner will become more relevant. At this specific point, we recommend that you live by a motto that helped us get through our divorces: **save your kids, and save your credit.** Another rule we lived by is: leave through the front door, not the back. What this means is: have the hard conversations, tell your partner you need to move on. Don't try to end the relationship by behaving so poorly they leave you, for example.

From John Negley, Family and Divorce Lawyer

John answered a few questions for us that could help.

1. 54% of all marriages end in divorce. As a divorce attorney, why is this number so high? JN: Obviously divorces happen for a host of reasons, but the overwhelming reason that I see is that people are increasingly self-centered and selfish. We see this at all levels including more parents making decisions based on what is in their best interest to the exclusion of those around them including their minor children . Social media has also had a strong influence on this with many thinking that "the grass is greener on the other side. . ."

2. Some divorces are amicable, but it seems most are not. When one is thinking a divorce might be best, how should they prepare and what things should they do to protect themselves. JN: First seek the advice of an attorney who specializes in this

area of the law. In California and many other states, attorneys can obtain a specialization designation from the state bar. Second, make sure you have a complete inventory of all assets and debts. Many have no clue what their financial situation is. Make sure you know where the community assets - and debts are. Third, don't act rashly. This is a big decision and one that should not be made flippantly. Seek marital counseling in order to avoid going down this road. Many people trade spouse number one with three problems for spouse number two who has five different problems from the first spouse. The divorce rate is high, but it gets higher the more times they get divorced. (See stats on this). Do EVERYTHING you can to reduce the effects of this divorce on your minor children. You will get through this largely unscathed. This is not always true for the minor children. Read books on how to do this as a nasty divorce can have lasting effects on your kids future relationships. Children will grow up to be happier, healthier, more self-confident and successful if the parents can "play nice" and co-parent in the best interest of the children. Lastly, consideration mediation or a collaborative approach to keep things out of court. This requires both parties to have reasonable expectations. Mediation is cheaper and less contentious which may allow you to still be friends or at least decent co-parents at the conclusion of this process.

3. When finding an attorney, how should one go about finding the best attorney for them? (because it seems all attorneys are not equal). JN; Find someone who specializes in Family Law and not a "Jack of all trades and master of none." Call your local bar association for referrals and look for someone

who has a state bar specialization designation. Get personal referrals and look for good online reviews - although not always definitive. Interview them and make sure that they are a good fit and read your retainer carefully. Check to see if they have had any discipline by the state bar. However, personal referrals and/or their reputation in the community is very telling. Ask connections that may work in the courthouse as word gets around who does a good job and who is just in it for the money.

4. How does one go about protecting their children when going through a divorce? JN: This is largely influenced by how the two parents treat one another in private and in public. Even very young kids notice and can tell by your body language how you feel about the other side. Read books on co-parenting. Take a co-parenting class. Take the high road in making decisions on co-parenting. Treat your ex with respect, even though you may not love each other. Go through this process in a way that will allow you to dance with your ex at your children's wedding because this approach is NOT just until they reach the age of 18. Get your children in therapy to assist them with going through this process, even if you don't think they need it.

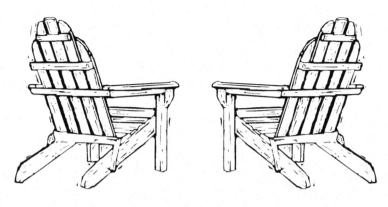

THE CAPACITY TO BE CLOSE

(INTIMACY)

Through conversations with friends and other couples we've noticed that the word "intimacy" doesn't appear to have a common definition. Most people think of intimacy as something sexual, or a state that can be achieved through sex. There can also be a misconception that if a couple is having sex it means they are experiencing intimacy in the relationship.

Sex and intimacy are two different things. For the purpose of this chapter, we are defining intimacy as: the capacity for closeness between two people.

According to therapist Alyssa Mancao, LCSW, "fostering a sense of closeness in any relationship (romantic or otherwise) requires a combination of four main types of intimacy: emotional, mental, spiritual, and physical."

A question to ask yourself is: what does it mean for me to be emotionally/mentally/spiritually intimate with my partner? Furthermore: when do I feel most intimate with my partner, and what is happening when I feel this way? We highly encourage you to make a list of your observations, and to examine how they change over time.

For some people, curling up on the couch and binge-watching Netflix can be extremely intimate, especially if they grew up in households where they always felt pressure to engage/perform.

However, if watching movies on the couch is the only way this couple bonds, they run the risk of gradually losing intimacy over time. The same goes for couples that enjoy going out for wine or cocktails together, for example. Over time, the activity that may have created a sense of bonding can lose its potential for intimacy, if it is the only way intimacy is created. The same goes for sex: if you only express intimacy physically, you run the risk of feeling deeply disconnected from your partner in the event that one or both of you experience a loss of sex-drive (due to illness, mental health, travel, etc)

It is therefore important to practice intimacy in all four areas: physically, emotionally, mentally, and spiritually. Furthermore Dr. Mancao explains that "experiential intimacy," as in, the intimacy derived from sharing new experiences with one another, is a fifth form of intimacy that serves to strengthen the relationship as a whole.

We encourage you to ask yourself "what do I need in order to feel available for intimacy?" The key is to be as honest with yourself as possible. Maybe you need a few hours to yourself before your date night. Maybe you need more than one date night a week, and you want one of those dates to take place outdoors. **Whatever it is, write it down, and bring the intimacy list to your partner during your monthly meetings.**

It is amazing, in the big picture, how unsuccessful we are at creating, and keeping strong relationships with our partners. Few of us are willing to admit how unhappy we are, and we seem to wait for something to change our relationship, which could be a tragic event, death of a loved one. Relationships need constant attention, if you aren't willing to put in the work and time, how can you possibly create a loving, kind, fulfilling and lasting relationship you can be proud of? There is nothing like being in a relationship that really works, it gets better and better as time goes on. If you want it, it's right here. We can attest to how beautiful a relationship can be with a little planning and thought. It's well worth it.

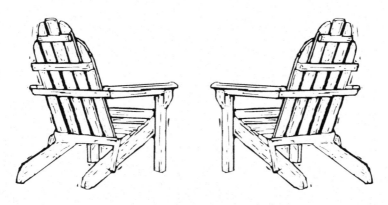

ACKNOWLEDGMENTS

We would like to acknowledge the people who helped us create this book. In addition to interviewing therapist Sarah Barrett Lepore, we interviewed couples to hear about the elements that made their relationship work. We encountered many pearls of wisdom in these interviews, which we are outlining here:

Sean and Bianca, who own a business together, attribute the success of their marriage to open communication, being willing to work out differences to arrive at common ground, and the commitment to listen to one another in order to ensure they both feel heard. The advice they would give to couples who are just entering a relationship is to be patient and to choose each other daily. They believe a healthy relationship is more important than a successful relationship, because the idea of success is usually based on external perception, whereas health is a reflection of an internal and holistic experience. According to them, a relationship consists of two imperfect people who come together in order to be the best version of themselves possible and to hold space for each other's evolution. And, they also believe that conflict can be an instrument of realignment: that conflict can act as a small earthquake that prevents a truly destructive earthquake.

Chris and Gary, who have been together for over thirty years, believe that the first year of marriage is the hardest. They attribute the success of their relationship to transparent communication, which means: saying what you really feel without holding back. They also believe having a strong foundation of friendship is important: they are best friends with common interests. The qualities they value most in one another are loyalty and honesty. Even when they were on different sides of the world and communication was difficult, they have never gone a day without speaking to one another, thus ensuring that their connection lives intact.

Liz and Joe, a couple based in Malibu, believe that being aligned in their love language is extremely important. At the end of the day they will have a cocktail and check in with one another. If there is something they want to talk about and process more deeply, they will walk along the beach. They describe this ritual as a spiritual recharge, and suggest seeking out beautiful and/or relaxing environments in order to process feelings and experiences that may require more attention. When it comes to advice they would give others, they suggest to beware of painting red flags white and to distribute the roles in a relationship in a way that adds value to the whole.

Morgan and Dannay, a couple based in Ventura, have a brilliant communication technique they use to check in with one another that helps them stay connected and gauge how they can best support each other, day-to-day. As part of their daily check-in, they will ask each other one simple question: "how's the weather up there?" In this context, "the weather" refers to their mental/emotional state. Some days can be sunny, whereas other days may be cloudy with a chance of rain. This simple question accomplishes several purposes. First, it creates the space for them to check in with themselves, internally, and evaluate how they are actually feeling. Second, this question is a direct invitation to authentically communicate how they are feeling to one another. Third, by asking this question, they create the opportunity to meet and show up to one another the way they need to be met, according to their weather.

Ultimately, there are as many ways to connect with one another as there are couples in the world. Whatever works for you, whatever ensures that you are heard and seen, that you hear and see, is what will deepen your relationship. We hope that what we have written resonates with you and helps you find your chairs, and that you continue to find the joy, love, and connection you are alive to experience.

Two years ago we met and started talking to Amanda Lezra about our idea of writing "Finding Your Chairs", and here we are. This could not have been done without the enormous support, thought and creativity that Amanda brought to our project. Amanda was the perfect person to work with, and we could not be more grateful.